W9-BZU-094

DATE DUE

DESIGNING THE FUTURE

Published by Creative Education
123 South Broad Street, Mankato, Minnesota 56001
Creative Education is an imprint of The Creative Company

Designed by Stephanie Blumenthal
Production design by Melinda Belter

Photographs by Priscilla Eastman, Nihat Iyriboz, Bernice Q. Johnson,
D.J. Lambrecht, Craig Lovell, Anthony Russo, Eugene G. Schulz and
Tom Stack & Associates

Library of Congress Cataloging-in-Publication Data

Halfmann, Janet.
Mosques / by Janet Halfmann.
p. cm. — (Designing the future)
Includes index.
Summary: Examines the history, design, construction, and uses of mosques
and describes some notable examples.
ISBN: 0-88682-690-X
1. Mosques—Juvenile literature. [1. Mosques.] I. Title. II. Series.

NA4670.H345   726'.2—dc21
1999   98-18205

First edition

9 8 7 6 5 4 3 2 1

CREATIVE EDUCATION

JANET HALFMANN

Mosques

DESIGNING THE FUTURE

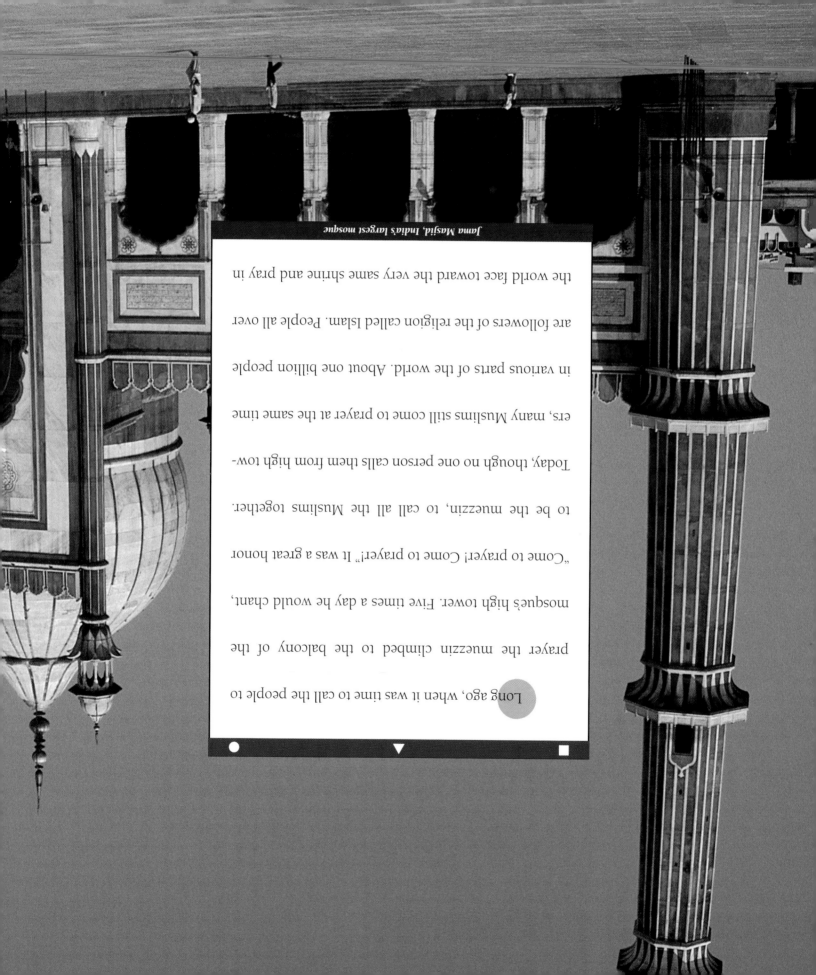

Long ago, when it was time to call the people to prayer the muezzin climbed to the balcony of the mosque's high tower. Five times a day he would chant, "Come to prayer! Come to prayer!" It was a great honor to be the muezzin, to call all the Muslims together.

Today, though no one person calls them from high towers, many Muslims still come to prayer at the same time in various parts of the world. About one billion people are followers of the religion called Islam. People all over the world face toward the very same shrine and pray in

Jama Masjid, India's largest mosque

the same language. In the United States they face east, and in China they face west. They all pray in Arabic as they look toward the Kaaba in Mecca.

The Kaaba shrine is located in the center of the Great Mosque in Mecca, Saudi Arabia. The shrine is believed to have been built first by Adam and then rebuilt more than 4,000 years ago by Abraham and his son Ishmael. People from Arabia and beyond flocked to this holy shrine. Religious stories tell that as years passed, people forgot the one God of Abraham and filled the Kaaba with many idols, or statues, of other gods. In the seventh century, Muhammad removed the idols and rededicated the Kaaba to God, called Allah

> The Kaaba is 50 feet (15m) tall and is covered with a black cloth with pure gold lettering. A container in which Abraham and Ishmael are thought to have mixed mortar for the building stands near the door.

Courtyard of Ibn Tulun, the oldest mosque in Cairo, Egypt

Entrance to the Blue Mosque, Istanbul, Turkey

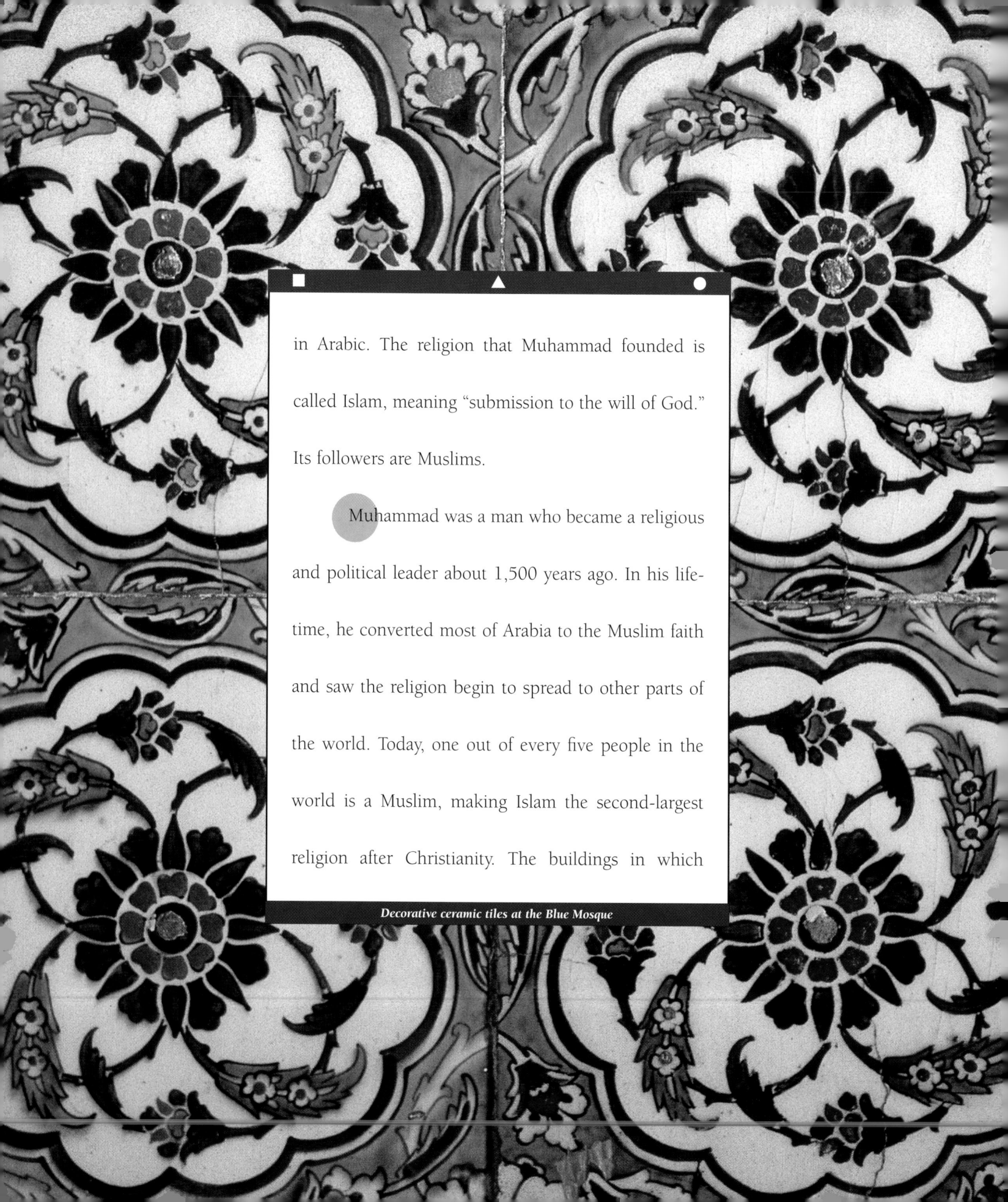

in Arabic. The religion that Muhammad founded is called Islam, meaning "submission to the will of God." Its followers are Muslims.

Muhammad was a man who became a religious and political leader about 1,500 years ago. In his lifetime, he converted most of Arabia to the Muslim faith and saw the religion begin to spread to other parts of the world. Today, one out of every five people in the world is a Muslim, making Islam the second-largest religion after Christianity. The buildings in which

Decorative ceramic tiles at the Blue Mosque

Muslims worship are called mosques. No matter what the design or location, all mosques developed from the first place of Muslim worship, Muhammad's house in Medina. His house was simple, with rooms along one side of a large courtyard. In front of the courtyard wall facing Mecca, he set up a shady place for worshippers by putting a palm leaf roof atop palm tree pillars. Muhammad's house was in the middle of the bustling city, just as many mosques are today. His house became known as a masjid or mosque—"a place where people bow down."

In Muhammad's day, one person called the others to prayer from the highest roof in the neighborhood. Later, high towers called minarets were added to mosques. A muezzin, or crier, climbed to the

About two million Muslims take part in the annual pilgrimage to Mecca. Pilgrims wear simple white garments so everyone appears equal. They circle the Kaaba seven times, pray, and then visit other holy sites.

balcony of the minaret to chant the call to prayer. Today, loudspeakers often broadcast this call, but the chant is the same, "There is no god but God, and Muhammad is the messenger of God. Come to prayer! Come to prayer!" The chant at dawn adds, "Prayer is better than sleep." Muslims are called to prayer five times a day. They can pray anywhere, but they gather at a mosque when they can. At noon on Friday, the Muslim holy day, all men are required to go to the mosque. Women are required to pray,

Entrance of the Pearl Mosque, Delhi, India

but they do not have to go to the mosque. Many women pray at home instead.

A mosque's entrance is often beautifully decorated. It separates the peaceful area inside from the noise of the city outside and reminds worshippers that prayer is a doorway to God. Shoes are left at the door, then people wash their faces, arms, hands, and feet under faucets or in a fountain. Washing is a sign of a clean body and soul. At the Badshahi Mosque at

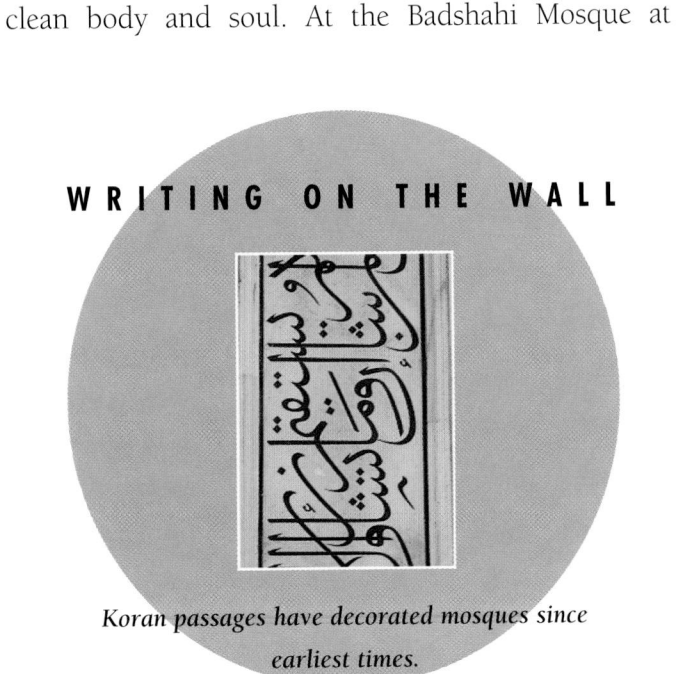

WRITING ON THE WALL

Koran passages have decorated mosques since earliest times.

Taj Mahal entrance

Lahore, Pakistan, the marble-covered domes of the mosque are reflected in the great courtyard pool. The inside of the mosque is a large open area; the only furnishings are rugs and hanging lamps. There is no altar or choir. The prayer room is wider than it is long because everyone stands side by side in long rows. Women pray in their own rows behind the men or in a separate area of the mosque.

Jama Masjid balcony, red sandstone

All worshippers face the same wall, called the qibla wall. It gets its name from the stone (qibla) that was placed in Muhammad's house after his death to mark the spot where he stood to pray. In the center of the qibla wall is a hollowed-out space with an arch at the top called a mihrab, or prayer niche, indicating the direction of Mecca. The imam, the man who leads the prayers, stands in or in front of the mihrab. It is the most decorated spot in the mosque and often has

CERAMICS

Potters in Iznik, Turkey, invented a way of painting bright colors on white tiles covered by a shiny, clear glaze. Mimar Sinan used tile with their flowers and arabesques in mosques that he designed, especially the lavish Mosque of Rüstem Pasha in Istanbul.

Pearl Mosque

Interior of the Green Mosque, Bursa, Turkey

passages from the Koran done in beautiful writing called calligraphy. One of the most unique and decorative mihrabs is in Spain's Great Mosque in Córdoba.

To the right of the mihrab is the minbar, or pulpit, which has a staircase leading to a small platform. Minbars are made of wood, stone, or marble, and are often elaborately

decorated. The minbar comes from a three-stepped chair that Muhammad sat on when he preached so everyone could see and hear him. Now at the Friday noon prayer, the imam stands on the stairs to preach a sermon—but he doesn't stand on the top step because that is the sacred spot reserved for Muhammad.

Minaret at Taj Mahal

Often many of the surfaces inside a mosque—the mihrab, walls, pillars, and dome—are completely covered with elaborate designs in wood, plaster, painted tiles, or mosaics. The designs repeat in seemingly unending patterns, to make it seem like the pillar or wall is not there at all but perhaps a magnificent flower garden instead. Favorite design elements are flowers, circles and other mathematical shapes, and passages

their foreheads as they pray.

Some large mosques have another platform called a dikka, where a few worshippers stand so they can see the imam and follow his actions, which every-one does with perfect timing. Near the dikka, an ornately carved stand holds the Koran. On the floor are reed mats or carpets with brightly colored designs because worshippers kneel and touch the ground with

Interior of Amr Ibn el Asi Mosque, Cairo, Egypt

While the inside of a mosque is usually highly decorated, the outside is generally plain. Any outside decoration is usually on the dome, minaret, or entrance. Often, one has to enter the courtyard to see the mosque's decorated entrance. Outside decoration is done in the same beautiful way as the inside, with unending patterns in wood, stone, colorful painted

from the Koran. These designs are often called arabesques. Human and animal figures aren't used in mosques because only God can create a living creature.

Main entrance at Selimiye Mosque, Turkey

tiles, or mosaics. Often the patterns include passages from the Koran. The tile-covered domes in Isfahan, Iran, are some of the most colorful. Domes rise in many different shapes. Some are rather flat and others are round and full. Some are smooth and others are textured or ribbed.

Mosques' appearances can vary a great deal because Islam is practiced in so many different countries. For example, in the desert of Arabia, a mosque

DECORATION

This gradually-tapered design gives the impression of soaring into the sky.

Courtyard at Süleymaniye Mosque, Istanbul, Turkey

Hagia Sophia, Istanbul, Turkey

with an open courtyard and flat roof is perfect, but in some parts of Turkey where it rains often, a covered building with a domed roof works better.

Despite their differences, most large mosques are of three basic types. The most common is the Arab or courtyard style. The earliest style, it was adopted throughout the Muslim world in the first five centuries of Islam. This style of mosque has columned halls surrounding a courtyard. A large prayer hall is at one end, which sometimes has one or more small domes—especially in front of the mihrab. Examples are the Great Mosque of Damascus in Syria (709–715), the oldest existing monumental mosque in the world; the Mosque of Ibn Tulun in Cairo, Egypt (876–879), with its spiral stone minaret and marble and gold mosaic–covered mihrab; Spain's Great Mosque in Córdoba (785–787), one of the best-known monuments

City of the Dead, Cairo, Egypt

White onion-shaped domes

ber in front of the mihrab. The iwan entrances are often covered in colorful tiles with elaborate patterns or passages from the Koran. Examples are the Masjid-i Jami in Isfahan, Iran (late 11th century), the complex of Sultan Hassan in Cairo, Egypt (1356–63), and the Royal Mosque in Isfahan, Iran (17th century).

The Ottoman or Turkish mosque is yet another style. It appeared in the 13th century. Its main element is a large central dome, framed by slender

of Islam and famous for its red and white double horseshoe-shaped arches; and the African Sankore Mosque (now used as a university) in Timbuktu, Mali (14th–15th centuries).

Another basic type is the Iranian style seen in western Iran beginning in the late 11th century. A mosque in this style has four large arched halls called iwans that open into a central courtyard. The prayer hall iwan is much larger and leads to a domed cham-

Mosque of Mohammed Ali, Cairo, Egypt

Taj Mahal in Agra, India

minarets. This type of mosque appeared in all the lands that came under Ottoman rule, but its masterpieces such as Selimiye at Edirne and Süleymaniye at Istanbul were created in the 16th century by Mimar Sinan, the greatest architect in Turkish history.

In 1550, Sinan started work on the magnificent royal Süleymaniye Mosque for Sultan Süleyman the Magnificent, ruler of the mighty Ottoman Empire that included half of the civilized world. This mosque in the capital of Constantinople (now Istanbul) was to be the largest in the empire to show the greatness of Islam and the power of its ruler. The two tallest minarets are more than 210 feet (64 m) tall—higher than a 20-story skyscraper.

In China, mosques often have a pagoda minaret, a tower with a curving roof at each level. The whole complex is enclosed by a wall. An example is the Niu Jie (Ox Street) Mosque at Beijing, built in 1362.

The Great Mosque in Mecca, Saudi Arabia, is Islam's holiest mosque because it holds the Kaaba, the shrine most sacred to all Muslims. All Muslims are expected to make a pilgrimage to Mecca once in their lifetime if possible. The Great Mosque started as a small roofless temple with walls of stone. Now, it is the largest mosque in the world, holding 700,000 worshippers.

The Prophet's Mosque in Medina, Saudi Arabia, was originally Muhammad's house, and thus became the first mosque. It is the burial place of

Tiled dome of Isfahan

Mosque of Sultan Süleyman, Istanbul, Turkey

Muhammad and the second holiest place in Islam. Today, this mosque in Saudi Arabia is 100 times its original size, and holds 500,000 people. It has 2,017 columns covered in Italian marble and 208 stained glass windows.

The Dome of the Rock is Islam's third holiest site and its earliest surviving monument. Built in 685–692 in Jerusalem, Israel, it is one of Islam's most beautiful buildings. The eight-sided marble building is decorated with vivid blue, yellow, and white tiles and crowned with a large gold dome. At the mosque's center is the rock on which Muhammad and his winged horse Buraq are believed to have stood before being raised up to heaven.

The Royal Mosque in Isfahan, Iran, is one of the most stunning buildings in the world. No surface is undecorated. Brilliantly colored glazed tiles, mostly blue, cover its great dome and four iwans. The entrance iwan is the most magnificent, with holy sayings, peacocks, stars, and vines. The mosque was built by Shah Abbas I in 1611–1638.

There are Blue Mosques in Tabriz, Iran; Cairo, Egypt; and Istanbul, Turkey. They all got their names from their blue tile decorations. When Sultan Ahmet I was having the Blue Mosque built in Istanbul, he

F O O T W E A R

Wooden "clogs" are used to cover the soles of the feet of anyone coming to worship at a mosque in Kenya.

Azhar Mosque, Cairo, Egypt

ordered the potters at Iznik not to sell tiles to anyone else until his mosque was finished. More than 20,000 tiles in 50 designs cover the interior of his mosque built in 1609–1617.

The Taj Mahal Mosque in Agra, India, is part of a complex that includes the Taj Mahal, considered the jewel of Islamic architecture.

Some Muslims use a special prayer rug with a mihrab-shaped design on it at home. The rug is placed on the floor or bare ground with the top of the mihrab facing Mecca. Some prayer rugs have two or three mihrabs side by side and are known as "brother rugs."

The beautiful complex was built by Shah Jahan in memory of his beloved wife, whom he affectionately called Mumtaz Mahal, meaning "ornament of the palace."

Work began on the monument in 1632 and took 20,000 workers from India and central Asia 22 years to complete. The Taj Majal is built

Domes of the Blue Mosque

Dome of the Rock, Jerusalem

completely of polished white marble, and decorated inside and out with calligraphy and flowers. The mosque is of red sandstone and has the three onion-shaped domes typical of mosques in India and nearby countries.

The Might of Islam Mosque at Delhi, India, was the first built in India in 1193. The courtyard-style mosque used building material from the ruins of temples. The mosque's towering Qutab Minar minaret rises 238 feet (73 m) high. The red sandstone and marble minaret was built not only to deliver the call to prayer, but stood as a victory tower and symbol of the new religion.

Small pavilion mosque, Turkey

Today, mosques are being built in every country of the world. One of the largest mosques in the United States is the Islamic Cultural Center in New York City, completed in 1991. This modern mosque looks like squares built upon squares. The pink granite building is topped with a large copper-covered dome and has a missile-like minaret. The building sits crooked so that its mihrab can face Mecca. In Canada, the Taric Islamic Centre in Toronto, built in 1991, is an elegant contemporary mosque.

A mosque along the Red Sea

Restored rural mosque

Hagia Sophia in Istanbul, Turkey

Some mosques of today combine the old and the new. For example, the design of the Grand Hassan II Mosque in Casablanca, Morocco, completed in 1993, imitates the great architecture of the 11th century. But the huge pink mosque has computerized loudspeakers, video screens, lighting systems, and even a laser beam that points the way to Mecca. A Muslim can enter a mosque anywhere in the world and feel at home. The majority of mosques built today, whether traditional or modern, include a dome and a minaret, which have become universal symbols of Islam. The mihrab will always point to the Kaaba in Mecca, and fellow worshippers will pray together in the same Arabic language—just as they did centuries ago in Muhammad's house in Medina.

Interior of Süleymaniye Mosque

I N D E X

Minarets on the Taj Mahal

32